# Dog
# Psalms

Prayers my dogs have taught me

*Herbert Brokering*

MONARCH
BOOKS
Oxford, UK, & Grand Rapids, Michigan, USA

Originally published in the United States of America by Augsburg Books in 2003.
Reproduced by permission.

First published in the UK in 2009 by Monarch Books
an imprint of
Lion Hudson plc
Wilkinson House, Jordan Hill Road,
Oxford OX2 8DR, England
Email: monarch@lionhudson.com
www.lionhudson.com/monarch

ISBN: 978-1-85424-936-4
e-ISBN: 978-0-85721-390-7

Photos: Stockxchange, Roger Chouler

A catalogue record for this book is available from the British Library

Printed and bound in the UK, August 2015, LH26

# Dog Psalms

To Dear Isobel ~ enjoy!

Love,
Shirl xx

**Dedicated to dogs who have helped me pray:**

*Rex*
*Tippy*
*Peggy Ann*
*Scamper*
*Schnappsie*
*Spitz*
*Bruno*
*Millie*
*Blaise*

# CONTENTS

PART ONE

Dog Psalms

# Dog Psalms

# PART ONE

# Introduction

I know dogs in my life the way I know people and cats and trees and landscapes. Dogs are in my mindscape and help shape my thoughts, feelings, and prayer life. Dogs have taught me attributes I feel in myself when reflecting and praying. Dogs have shown me the spirit of being loyal, glad, overwhelmed, protective, committed, vigilant, patient, kind, energetic, discerning, forgiving. Unfolding these attributes of dog life opens my own spiritual being. My relationship with dogs mirrors my relationship with God. The title of this book might have been *Dear God, I Am Dog*.

In *Dog Psalms* the reader can use a dog's attributes to speak to God. It is a natural connection. Like a dog, I, too, wait and watch. Waiting and watching is a silent power, a gift in me. I wait for what I want, hope for, long for, need. I wait for what is next, for company coming, a voice on the phone, a word from the doctor. I watch for those who are away. Dear God, I pray in my waiting and watching. You have given me the gift of time. You have told me later, tomorrow, next year, later, later, later. You are my good master.

Who are the dogs I have known best? First, there was Rex, who lay in the sun with me on the cellar door of our parsonage in rural Nebraska. Rex's thoughts were my thoughts, and his ways were mine. I knew every flea on his body seventy years ago, and I cared for him as my mother cared for me.

Tippy and Peggy Ann, spotted terriers, were mother and daughter. I braided them collars and harnesses. They were in my homemade circus, under a tent where I was most often alone, watching, marvelling, in awe. This was a time before dog foods; Tippy and Peggy Ann ate our best scraps from the table. I cooked them porridge made of ground feed and wanted them to love it as I loved my porridge.

There were highs of births, scampering puppies; there were lows of giving puppies away, saying goodbye, dog burials. Then came life in the city and new dogs from dog pounds, especially Scamper, a Japanese spaniel from Louisiana. I experienced the spirit of joy, wisdom, melancholy, faithfulness, and adoration inside with each new member of the family.

Schnappsie, a dachshund in Detroit, taught me to relax, wiggle, welcome, snuggle, stretch, sleep. A white spitz in the Haeckel parsonage taught me that dogs nip, yip, protect, and say, "This is mine," just as my siblings and I did at home. I saw Spitz and I saw myself.

Going to the Cronick home in Byron, Nebraska, was a high point. There was a bark of Bruno, a Newfoundland whose voice would have rung like an echo through the Swiss Alps. Each visit woke a dream in me to be a rescue dog in the mountains, searching for lost people and bringing them food and drink around my collar.

Millie is a dog who now visits hospitals and homes, walking corridors, greeting people in wheelchairs or on beds. She wears ribbons and hats and helps people smile who often lose their laughter. Some say she is an angel, some say a minister. Millie believes she is Dog.

*Dog Psalms* is about what dog lovers have learned from watching the best friend lying at their feet. These teachers

wiggle and wag, snuggle, chase sticks, beg, depend on others for life, and exchange everything for lifelong commitments of faithfulness and love.

*Dog Psalms* is also about the human spirit, yours and mine. The readings are meant to help us speak out loud to our Master. We wiggle, we guard, we wait, we give, we hope, we hunt, we dig, we growl, we forgive, we beg, we stray, we whine, we jump, we snoop, we cuddle, we nudge, we pant, we charm, we heal. And our Master watches and loves us through it all.

Herbert Brokering

# I trust

**I am dog.** I am loyal.

Your trust is in me. You help me grow my trust. More and more we belong to each other. I pledge allegiance to you, as you have to me. When you double your faithfulness to me, I triple mine to you. I lean on you when I cannot stand by myself. When you have need, I will hold you. I am willing to help and to be helped. Your trust grows my loyalty. I depend on your dependability. Trust was planted in me long ago in the womb. Our trust will have no end. I depend on your kindness for a good life. I am dog and I am loyal. I need your faith for my faith.

# Dear God,

*You have given
me your trust.
Loyalty is in me.
I am yours as you
are mine. In a
storm, I lean
on you and you
hold me. You
are my anchor;
in doubt
you are my
hope. There
is no clear*

*line between us to keep us apart.
You surround me and are inside me. You are above
and below and beside me. Your faithfulness gives me
faith.*

# I wiggle

**I am dog.** I love you.

My whole being shows you my affection. With eyes and lips and paws and tongue, I love you. I assume with my whole self that you love me too. I wiggle and wag and jump and climb and pant for you to love me. I am dog. I feel innocent even after proven guilty. I love you unconditionally, believing you love me the same. I am dog. The tides of the oceans are in me. I wiggle as I ride waves, hear love calls of ancient forests, feel the kiss of a wisp of wind. I have a spirit that runs through all times.

# Dear God,

My spirit wiggles
in me. I dance in
my heart when I
feel your closeness.
I cannot hold my
feelings still. Your
spirit runs through
me like a living
stream, a slow rhythm, and with you I am young.
You keep me alive with goodness from the earth and
the heavens. You find the good in me. You move me
with your joy.

# I plead

**I am dog.** My eyes sometimes look far away, search skies, sweep the horizon.

My eyes sometimes look to you, inside of you, through you. With my eyes I plead. My eyes meet your eyes and hold you, fix you, ask you, capture you. My heart can wrap around you, fix you, ask you, capture you. My heart can see my need, my want, my hope. Then your heart so you can see my need, my want, my hope. Then your heart. I can stare into your spirit. The deep I am in your heart. I can stare into your spirit. The deep silence in my eyes is stronger than my bark. I can bury my eyes in your eyes until we find tears. I can plead until you out-plead me. We hold each other in our eyes.

# Dear God,

*You see me plead with all my heart. I beg and do not hold back. I want, I wish, I need, I hope in front of you. I am careless in asking favours. I bury myself in you while you hold me in your eyes. I fix my thoughts on you until you capture me, quiet me, silence me. Your loving silence and touch hold me still.*

# I skip

**I am dog.** I can flood with emotion, fill with sudden happiness.

I tremble with affection when you come home. If I am asleep when you come, I stretch, skip, hurry, feel more awake than ever. My body is filled with power. I run go; I run, leap, swim. I am sometimes overwhelmed. I run in circles, jump, bark. I can be so overwhelmed I leap into

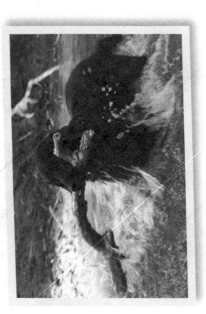

you, believing you will catch me, hold me, pet me, love me. When you surprise me, I can run faster to you than I ever ran, without even trying. I am dog and I overwhelm. I have no control over the spirit of my fullness.

## Dear God,

*My spirit runs in circles. Sometimes I fly, I climb, I flee. I go places beyond my daily life. I soar to heights eagles cannot ascend. I run races too fast for runners. I see beauty never painted, hear harmonies never written. I am a child who skips with my heart. You fill my life to the brim.*

# I guard

**I am dog.** I protect.

I know what is mine and yours. If it is yours it is like mine and I will guard it with my bark, my bite, my growl, myself. I will protect what I treasure with my whole being. My hair will stand on end, my body stiffen, my legs stretch strong, my eyes lock on what seems to be the enemy. I will judge the distance between the enemy and me; my voice will dictate the boundary I determine. If the enemy crosses my line, I will leap into a war dance meant to frighten. The dancing also makes me feel safe. I will lay down my life for what I strongly believe. I am dog. I protect.

# Dear God,

I keep up my guard. I say what is mine and I draw
a fence around it. I protect what is precious to me.
To guard and keep it safe, I raise my voice to make
myself bigger than I am. I study boundaries that keep
safe what is special. Show me the source of all my
strength. Remind me who guards me and who sees
me as precious. Then teach me how I am to defend.

## I commit

**I am dog.** I believe in unconditional love. I believe in true love to the end. I am a life-long lover who will lie at your feet, on the bed, by your chair, at your side. I am dog. I insist on your love. I will stay on a grave of a lover until my end. I believe in commitment. When we have chosen each other, I will be there for you, with plenty. Out of my heart flows life and love. You fill my life with abundance and I am fulfilled. Unconditional love is the highest gift. I am committed to love.

# Dear God,

*You gave me your love before I met you. You do not hold back or tease me with what you give. I am learning the strength of your unconditional love. You have shown me your commitment throughout my life; you have committed to me beyond this life. You have promised me love I cannot comprehend. You have made me a committed believer in commitment.*

# I watch

**I am dog.** I am vigilant. I watch with my eyes shut. I wake while I sleep. If a room is ours, I will keep it safe. If it is our garden, I will watch all four corners. Sometimes my vigilance is greater than my body weight, swifter than my leap. Sometimes my vigilance shrinks to a

whimper, whisper, silence. Yet I am there, and being there is also my vigilance. I will not flee readily. One growl and the enemy fears. One stir and the enemy steps back. I show my teeth and the enemy is sure I bite. I lift my head, I rise; the enemy runs away. I am a force, ready to prove my strength. I am dog. I wake quickly, vigilant. I watch out for you even when I rest.

# Dear God,

*I am vigilant even when my eyes are closed. I listen even when there is no sound. I look when there is nothing in sight. I keep watch with you. I wake quickly where there is need and will hurry to help without being told. I am vigilant, ready to stand or flee. I run in the dark and know where to find help. You do not leave me alone. I am ready to go, for you are already there.*

# I wait

**I am dog.** I am patient.

    I can be taught to wait. I do not prefer to wait in a long queue; I want to be the only dog waiting. If you are coming, I will wait, breathing deeply, half dreaming, wholly wishing. When I know you love me, I live for you with every breath. I bury my yearning deep inside and hide it in my sleeplessness. I toss and turn and wait until you are here. I wait for you sometimes while singing, sometimes while whimpering, howling, wanting with all my heart. I can wait loud or soft. I can wait through long night watches. I will wait without end, knowing I am wanted. I am dog, willing, patient. Waiting prepares me for your presence.

# Dear God,

*You have given me the gift of waiting. Like a child, I wait with my whole body, mind, and soul. I wait for seasons, they go; I wait for another, it comes. I wait for days to dawn, nights to darken, seeds to break open, fruit to fall. As I wait I learn the gift of patience and the joy of surprise. While I wait I find myself in your presence. I wait for you, and in waiting I see you are here, waiting.*

# I give

**I am dog.** I am kind.

When you come home, I will give you my full attention. I will give you my place, my time, my whole day, myself. While you heal, I will comfort, lick your hand, be still, stay near you. If you need, I will give you a night watch. I will be glad when you are glad, run when you run, leap when you leap. I want to be with you, see your laughter, feel your kindness. When you give abundantly, I think of thanks. See how I gulp the food you give, lap the cool

drink, come running before you finish calling me? I want you
to witness my acts of kindness. My kindest word is in my
deed.

## Dear God,

*I am thankful for the wonder of giving. I know
the feeling of breaking a biscuit in two to share it,
of wrapping something ordinary with a bow, of
handing on a good story as legacy, of dividing my
time with another. Your loving kindness is in me,
and I will do acts of mercy I do not plan. Your giving
is becoming a habit in me. I am learning kindness.*

# *I hope*

**I am dog.** I expect a treat.

It is not that I always deserve, but I expect a treat, a hug, a pat, a good word, a compliment. I expect you to treat me like the dog I truly am, the dog inside me who is even greater than the one people know. The dog inside is more loyal, more watchful, more playful than some have seen me. You make me feel worthy of a treat; you are the one who spoils me, satisfies me, makes me expectant, hopeful. You have taught me to expect my just reward. You want me to be treated to a treat. I receive over and over. I am full of hope from head to toe.

# Dear God,

*The gift of hope is built into my world. There are paths and windows and doors open to what is coming. You have taught me to expect and wish and ask and hope. You give to me over and over and over, so I know there is more and more. Hope is at the edge of each night and day, each season and place. As a bloom is in the seed, so your hope is stored in me. Unfold the hope in me.*

# I laugh

**I am dog.** I am ready to be happy.

I am designed to wag, smile, laugh, radiate joy. A glance, a touch, a morsel, a whistle, and I feel the good run through me. Take me for a walk or run, save me from the cold, be near me, play with me, and I will be glad. I can show my delight with a shiver, a closing of my eyes, a single bark. Those who love me know the moment I shine, grin, laugh out loud. I can save my joy, hold it in; it can explode, knock you down. One tiny word, one wink, one hug can make me happy all day. I am glad for simple things. Inside me is a feeling waiting to laugh.

## Dear God,

*You make us laugh. Creation is full of joy. The sea and earth and heavens rejoice. There is a humour on earth that we catch, and so we laugh and tease and are glad. We wink and smile and whistle and* 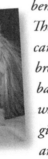 *bend over laughing. There is a joy in us we cannot contain. Fun breaks out; shouts and barks and meows and warbles explode. You give us comedies and anthems and parades and celebrations. You have created life with a strong sense of laughter.*

# I hunt

**I am dog.** I was born to hunt.

I sniff the ground, the air, the wind, the sky, the familiar, the new. I watch the horizon, the brush, the leaves to know what moves. I am predator of rabbits, squirrels, pheasants, ducks, bees, or bits of table food. I hunt what is near and what I never ever find, which sleeps like a dangling carrot inside my ancestry. I will trace sounds you cannot hear, smells you cannot smell, sights that are specks in the sky. I will follow the trail for miles. I was born in the wild but trained to repress, bred to repress. I am always on the hunt. I follow the Geiger counter inside me. I am dog. I know my target.

# Dear God,

*I hunt what I never find. I seek what I never see. I am on the go, looking, digging, uncovering. You take me where I have never been, and I return to places as though I have not seen them before. My world stays new; there is a vista before me, and then another. I come to one horizon and there is the next. Inside me is an eye that needs to seek and find what is hidden before me.*

# I chase

**I am dog.** I chase.

I chase to catch, to win, to conquer. My eye will not leave the chase. I will spin, jump, climb, dig, sprint in pursuit. I am made to chase. I chase to play. I snatch balls in mid air, dive after sticks in deep water, twist and soar to capture Frisbees. If no one will throw for me, I will chase my tail, my shadow. I will snap at the wind, a falling autumn leaf, snow in flight. But I chase best with a friend, an audience, someone cheering, shouting my name. They know I am chasing, chasing, chasing. I am dog. I have goals to catch.

# Dear God,

*My spirit is on a chase. I run through meadows into summer wind, follow clouds fast on the move, reach to catch a dancing snowflake, look up at migrant flights, and follow a tumbling leaf to the ground. There are paths I run to find a rising sun, streets I walk to meet the same friends, prayers I say each day, and words I read again and again and again. I chase old and new routes and know when I have caught what I am hunting. I have chosen what it is I chase most.*

# I dig

**I am dog.** I am filled with curiosity.

I want to know what is not my business. I dig. I plough under leaves, poke through a toy box, and route out a clump of rags to find the spirit of what is not there. Without any excuse, I ravage a tiny earth hole where there is neither mouse nor bird nor chipmunk in hiding.

I am eager to discover what has long been gone, save the scent. I can test a spider from more sides with my paws than Picasso could with a brush. When something is just out of reach, I am overcome with a wanting spirit. I will return again and again until my curiosity is satisfied. My need to seek and find is relentless. I have an inquiring spirit.

## Dear God,

*I dig. I want to know. You have made me curious. I want to learn more. I want to know the sky by heart, know the planets by name and point them out to my friends. I want to learn another language to hear the thoughts inside other people. Thank you for those who discover what has long disappeared, which we need to know. Give me the mind to stay with things that are important, so I find their meaning and beauty.*

# I growl

**I am dog.** I growl.

I growl to possess, to protect, to ward off, to own. Growling is my act of diplomacy. It is my warning, my first signal of danger ahead, my good will. I growl to stop confrontation so I need not bite. My growl is greater than my anger. With it, I create the distance I need between us. Growling is often as far as I go with harm and defence. After growling I am known to run off, hide, duck, or wag as an alternative approach. In growling, I test the danger, estimate the harm, interface with foe or friend. Growling is my checkpoint. I am diplomat, I measure respect, I watch over peace. I am an ambassador for good will.

## Dear God,

*I growl. I growl to ward off danger; my growl is a shield around me. I growl to create a distance that makes me safe. My growl gives me a little time to understand what I am to do next. I do not want the fight; I want the peace. Move me quickly from growling to grace, turn my confrontation into good will. Make me an ambassador of understanding.*

# I shine

**I am dog.** I am bred. My lineage is celebrated. I am known for my teeth, called by a Latin name. People study my pedigree, compare me with ancestors, consider my descendants. I may have a lineage that begins in China or Germany. I may be famous for mixtures some call Heinz. Pictures of my kind are coloured by school children, published in books. I look like breeds before me. Yet with my distinctiveness, I win blue ribbons. I am created after my own kind. In my family are

traits hunters want, children love, shepherds buy, police train. I am made to be fierce, coy, shy, swift, gentle, strong, sweet. I have a mould not easily broken. I am dog. I have a lineage. My character is built for greatness.

## Dear God,

*I have a pedigree. I have value. I am somebody. People know me a certain way. Yet I am like no one else. There is a lineage I own that is my own. My traits qualify me for a lifelong work. People want me for who I am, how I feel and act, what I am able to do. Unfold in me the lineage I have inherited that makes me special. Help me to be what I am to be. I am glad to have my life.*

# I work

**I am dog.** It is my nature to work.

I can guard property, guide sheep, attack foes, find wrongdoers, point out fowl, jump through hoops. I am good at my work. I am happy when visiting sick, walking from old to young, wagging, snuggling, schmoozing, getting treats. I live for pulling sledges through snow, corralling scattered sheep in valleys, finding survivors in rubble. My nature is to work. You will know me by my good work. I am at my best when on duty. You need me. I am worth my bread.

# Dear God,

*There is business to do in the world, and I will do some of the work. There are loads to pull, burdens to hold, sick to heal, rivers to forge. Here I am; I am worth my bread. There are lost to find, races to win, people to cheer, poor to feed. There is business to do in the world; some of the work is mine. Show me the work I am able to do. Guide me when I volunteer.*

# I miss

**I am dog.** I miss you.

If you are gone too long, I grow listless and lose my glow. I feel shaggy inside. When I finally see you, I run to meet you more than halfway. I overwhelm you with my signs of missing you. Missing you stores a power in me that explodes in your presence. If I am old, I act young again. If I hurt, I feel no pain. If I am weak, I grow strong again. As I miss you, I prepare to give you everything I am, in a flashing moment. I miss you the way I think you miss me. I do not ask how much you miss me; I believe how much you miss me.

## Dear God,

*I long for someone. I miss people. I miss those I knew and will not see. I miss those I know and are not here. I miss some I have never met. I miss some before they leave me. I miss the places I know by heart, every aroma, every tree, every flower, every nook and cranny. You have made me with the gift to miss, to long for, to stay connected to what is never finished. When I miss, I feel a great power leaving. I wait for its return, and then I will dance.*

# I forgive

**I am dog.** I forgive without asking for forgiveness.

I will forgive before you are ready to receive my look, my lick on your hand. I do not bargain forgiveness; I do not

make a deal. You are forgiven even before you harm or shout or neglect or ignore. Tomorrow is a new day. Tonight is already a new time. The sun will not set on my anger. I forgive you for I am yours and you are mine. We agreed without a signed document. You can hold me to words I cannot say, to a sentence I cannot write. Hold me to who I am. I am dog and I forgive. Forgiving feels right. I do not ask why. I will not sleep with a grudge.

## Dear God,

*I forgive. I will not go to sleep with a grudge. I do not carry anger with me for long. I know the strength and peace inside forgiving. I believe forgiveness weakens a battle line, erases wrinkles in the spirit, brings relief to my mind. I forgive and chains fall, foe becomes a friend, a family relaxes, children hug and sing and play again. Forgiveness makes possible change, a time to grow, telling the truth, acts of kindness, reconciliation. Your forgiveness is in me.*

# I stray

**I am dog.** I stray.

I follow what I want for a while, then lose where I am and what I was seeking. I wander off the path we walk each day, then make a bend that is new. If I cannot find my way back, you worry. You hunt for me. You post my name and picture and offer a high reward. Lost, I tear myself apart. Sometimes I run in frantic circles. I share the hurt of being lost. I am sorry that I stray, yet once found, I may stray again. You know I may stray again. I will listen for and hear your call. I am dog. I wait to be found. I will go far to be with you again.

# Dear God,

*You hunt me and find me when I stray. You know every turn I make, what I wander off to see, and when I am lost and cannot find home. You call my name and I hear your voice. If I am frantic, your voice does not leave me. You give laughter to loved ones when I return. So there is joy in the universe, and heavens, when something lost is restored. How is it that you give us the gift to wander so?*

# I nest

**I am dog.** I nest.

I turn and turn to lie down. I know the basket, the rug, the corner, the sofa. I make the place my safe nest. I nest like a bird, making sure my place is right. I nest where I can see you, feel you near, hear your voice, guard you. I nest in a ritual of comfort, knowing I am now home. My nest is mine, found and prepared through time. It is our place. The light is right, the mood is right, the spirit right, so I lay me down to rest. I nest, and all around me there is certain peace. I turn, lie down, I enter into your presence. This is our place.

# Dear God,

*I know my place of rest. It is our place, where I hear you best, where you are near and I am safe. You give me places that are my home, where my spirit is right, mind is right, mood is right. You* 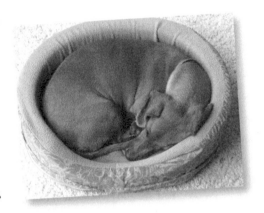 *see me turn this way and that way, inside, outside, until I find my nesting place. In all sounds and sights around and within, you show me how to stay where I am to find your presence. Thank you for our still places, they are holy.*

# I snuggle

**I am dog.** I snuggle.

I get close. I snuggle into your body, under your arms, into your lap, between your feet. I snuggle in your bed, into your eyes, into your presence. I snuggle into your voice, into your favourite chair, behind your pillow, beneath your book. I wrap myself around your heart. I am created to be close to you, with you, of you. I can snuggle so we are like one. When I move, you move. I sleep then you sleep. You wake then I wake. You stretch, I stretch. I snuggle to stay near when we are apart. You are more near than far. I feel your snuggle when you are away. I am absolutely loved.

# Dear God,

*I snuggle. I get close, stay near, get deep into your presence. I look for your words that make me safe, keep me close, love me. I look for your heart in all*

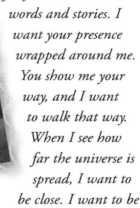

*words and stories. I want your presence wrapped around me. You show me your way, and I want to walk that way. When I see how far the universe is spread, I want to be close. I want to be under your arms, in your hands, and at your feet. You are more near than far.*

# I bluff

**I am dog.** I bluff, and I am good at it.

Though I may be small, I can make my bark far bigger than my bite. The situation determines the size of my bluff. I bluff to get attention. I bluff as a first line of defence. I am usually better at fencing than fighting. I use a bluff to talk to strangers, to know why they came, if they can be trusted. A bluff is like a peephole in a door, a safety chain before I open wide. A dog likes to know who is asking to come in. If I bluff the same people over and over, they will not believe me. I do not bluff those I trust most. I am dog. I am honest. I need truth to set me free.

## Dear God,

*I bluff. My bark is bigger than my bite. My bluff is the way I negotiate. My spirit fences. My spirit weighs my strength in the presence of what is new. I am cautious before I open myself to what I have never seen. I test the ice before I walk into the middle of everything. I bluff to find out where we stand, so we can talk. You make me grounded. I do not bite and will not fight. I am learning to trust.*

# I nudge

**I am dog.** I nudge.

I look to you for abundance, for more and more and more. I dig my nose into your hands. I know where to push so you feel the power of my nudge. When your hand is empty, I do not show disappointment. I stay to receive what I think is there for me. I stay so you feel my hope grow. I nudge to dream of what more you have. I can tell when the nudge is welcomed. I nudge and stay so you can nudge me back. To be close is often enough. Your presence is my peace. My nudge is a wish that you have heard me. When you nudge back, then I am in you. I am dog. I nudge, I receive. I am contented. I am at rest.

# Dear God,

*Stay close. You know I need more and more of what you give. I dig myself into your presence until I feel you hold me. I look for your promises. I bury myself into your mercy and might. You touch me, and I touch you back. Your presence is my peace. I nudge you, I find the palm of your hand, I am contented. You are here for me.*

# I pant

**I am dog.** I pant.

I pant when the sun is hot. I pant when I have run hard. I pant after a chase to catch what is thrown for me. I lay down at your feet a winner, exhausted. I pant for coolness, fresh water. I pant, I crave, I long violently for the mystery of life. I come to the water and drink. Throw me into the summer water and I come back to you, soaked, shaking myself dry. I am dog. I crave. I look to you. I am quenched. My heart is refreshed. My thirst is satisfied.

## Dear God,

*My soul pants for living water. I go through desert places and I thirst. I feel the coolness of a running stream, and I am refreshed and made glad. I lay me down beside still waters. My soul is restored. I yearn and I thirst for a drink that quenches my hunger, and I am satisfied. In your water I find life.*

# I heal

**I am dog.** I make well.

People tie a ribbon on me; they feel better. I wear a sweater, a jacket, a bonnet; children laugh and lose their pain. I catch a Frisbee; voices cheer me on. I roll over; crowds gather in awe. People give me compliments I do not understand, but I feel their words. Ones I love take me to visit people who are alone. We walk down corridors in a healing parade. I snuggle with sick from bed to bed. All ages kiss me, look me in the eye, tell me what they cannot say to each other. I know their souls, their hurt, their fear. I know the bark they need to hear. When people hold me, they are better than before. When I leave, people wave. We bless each other. I smile. I am dog, I am here to make well.

## Dear God,

*You bless me so I bless. You make me your own, and I carry your goodwill into the world. I have places where I go door-to-door, bed-to-bed, sick-to-sick. I bring good news, a smile, a touch, understanding, a flower, empathy. They are glad when I come. We pray. They wave when I leave. But it is not over. They wait and I return. I stay with them, and they with me, while we are apart. You give us this gift of real presence. I am here to be well.*

# PART TWO

# Introduction

God said: "let there be dog."

These psalms are focused toward "peace-making". The twenty-six devotions are prayers of peace. In this writing "dog" is guiding me to pray for kindness, reconciliation and the building of peace. If a "lily of the field" can guide me to be less anxious then why not "dog" be an example for peace-making.

Many dogs I have known help me feel and think toward peace: "If I have wounded you I will lick it and say I am sorry. I will sneak back to you, crawl back, come close, and touch you to make sure you know my heart. Say my name; do not be quiet when I repent. I know your reconciling voice. Touch me so I know we are making peace. Make me sure you will not permit a grudge to separate us. I am dog. We are face to face, heart to heart."

May these dog psalms show you more and more the many attributes of God embedded in creation. See in dog and tree and river and seed and wind and bird and sky the glory of God. May these psalms of the dog make you more and more a psalmist seeing all of life as language of God.

"I am dog. I forgive. A grudge will lead to isolation. Anger is my enemy; fear is a foe. I do not sleep well when we hurt. Forgiveness has the feel of stretching, a cool drink on a hot day, a warm blanket when chilled by rain, a safe pat after being chased by a predator." May Part Two of *Dog Psalms* help you see your dog in a new light.

Look again at your dog and pretend hearing: I am dog. I teach you the meaning of peace-building.

"Dear God, I know your word: Thou shalt not hold a grudge. Grudge is an enemy to peace-making. Forgiveness is stronger than fear and anger and grudge and harm. Forgiveness breaks the strength of sin."

May many lines in these readings open up insights and peaceful vistas.

"I am dog. I am committed to you. I will keep my promise to you. I will do what we have agreed. If needed I will suffer for you, and be wounded in your stead.... There is a tie that binds us which cannot be broken."

Dog Psalms

I wish it were written somewhere in the book of Luke,
"Consider the dog."

Herbert Brokering

# Adore

**I am dog.** I adore.
I look up with
more than admiration.
How often I have
nothing to say. I stare
for there is light
around you. You
are greater than I. I
know this and I feel
splendour. We each come

from two worlds into this one another world. I am
dog, made very good, but I am not the highest being. You
are beyond me, whom I serve and obey. I need someone to
whom I lift up my eyes. I dig a hole to sleep in; you build a
house with stairs. I claim a corner under a porch; you give me
a hand-sewn quilt on an oak floor. I lick an open wound to
heal; you drive me to a vet. I bark twice and jump in your lap;
you hold me warm, close your eyes and pray. I beg against a

screen cage in a kennel; you carry me home in a basket and repeat my name. I am learning to adore. I am dog. I look up and you are more than friend. I am at peace.

## Dear God,

*You made me to adore. I see beyond myself. I look in silence, admiring mountain majesty, springtime twigs and newborn fingerprints. My heart is dumbfounded by harvest time. I lift my eyes to hills with your children on all the earth who also live in awe. We all come with dim eyes; you heal our sight. You unveil and reveal as we stare side by side. You give rest and rain to just and unjust. You say who is perfect for you know our secret thoughts that we do not see in ourselves or in one another. You know what the old and infants do that makes for peace. You are a God of goodwill; we are created to adore, to look up and hear the song of peace and goodwill.*

# Test

**I am dog.** I test my limits.

I know the ways of freedom are tender and true. I go to the end of my boundaries; I know the property line. I accept limitations I cannot cross. I do not climb trees. I know my limits and will test them. If I climb to the tip of the branches I fall. I will try once. I accept that I am dog and learn to live within my limits. I do not like living on a leash. There are true limits in my nature. I will find my limits and not be confined. I will not chase a lion but I will run. I will not swim the ocean but I will enjoy water. I will not be a kangaroo or zebra. I will not attack an alligator or race a gazelle. I am dog; I will be glad to take a dog test. I will not study; I will pass the test for I am dog. Peace requires the truth.

# Dear God,

*You set limits for seas and for rays of the sun. You have marked borders in your creation and lines we are not to cross. You put a tree in the garden to test our faithfulness to you and all boundaries for behaviour. We are people warned and nations tested.*

*You ask questions true and false, you set limits in laws of nature and rules for life with each other. When obeyed we have peace. Help us live without a leash. We are to live so all win and none lose, all pass and none fail, all hope and none fear. Take from us the fear of failing and fill us with the hope of peace. Take us to the very edge of creating and the making of goodwill.*

# Respect

**I am dog.** I have rights; I require respect.

I am dog. I am made to do what dog does. My history informs my spirit. Being dog is a long story. In me lives a deep wish. It is my duty to obey what I am born to be. I like being dog. I like my face, my tail, and the markings in my colour, my hair. I like the way I walk, wag, wiggle, watch nature, romp, chase, am. I am dog and was born dog. I know the language of barking, the meaning of growling and howling. My story is a true story; my reasons are in me. I do as dog has done before me. People know me as dog, a living being. They look through chronicles to study me, respect me. I am dog, only dog, very dog. My nature is of old. There is none like me. I am what I am; I am dog. I cannot be otherwise.

## Dear God,

*I am made in your image. You breathed into
me breath and brought to life this person, this
body, mind, and spirit. You marked me before
my beginning with the traits of my ancestors. A
genealogy is in me from those long before me. As
recorded in scriptures I too am 'begat'. My spirit is of
old and in my mother's womb you knew me. In me
lives the miracle of being human. I have potential;
I have limitations. I have no wings and I cannot
breathe under water. I cannot fly with eagles or
swim through deep oceans with whales. I do not
bark; I cannot crow. I can reason, write, ask, ponder,
calculate, meditate, moderate, will, create goodwill
on earth. I know the language of being human. I
know our long story. Dear God, how you do give me
honour. I know the spirit of respect. I am made a
little lower than angels; so are we all.*

# Reconcile

**I am dog.** I let go of my wrath.

I do not nurture a grudge. I will wipe a slate clean. I do not plan warfare. See how close I stay by you. I expect you to not hold a fault against me. I am open to

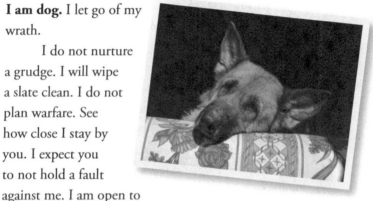

forgiveness. I look you in the eye and wag repentance. Stay with me eye-to-eye, heart-to-heart. Do not look away when I need to hear you voice. I nuzzle you and will not let the sun go down while anger is in me. If I have wounded you I will lick it and say I am sorry. I will sneak back to you, crawl back, come close, and touch you to make sure you know my heart. See me return before it is too dark. Say my name; do not be quiet when I repent. I know your reconciling voice. Touch me so I know we are making peace. Make me sure you will not permit a grudge to separate us. I am dog. We are face-to-face, heart-to-heart.

## Dear God,

*I do not ponder or plan retaliation. Wrath and warfare is my enemy. I see you in the eyes of others so we are one family. From a distance I feel the voice and touch of another nation. The sun does not set on my anger; in the dark I seek to forgive and to bless so I have no enemy. I will not use the dark to harm those who call me their foe. I will try for a truce even before warfare begins. You have given us the gift of conversation, the spirit of reconciling and the miracle of peace. I believe in the power of peace that surpasses understanding. Wrath is the work of war. Reconciliation is the work of peace.*

# Excel

**I am dog.** I can do more, still more and still more.

I can excel. I am capable of finding land mines without being harmed. I am careful. My every step shows watchfulness, a special gift, and my excellence. I can capture drug dealers with my nose. I have a gift in me to do heroic rescues. I am dog. I can change the beat of your heart, lick to heal an open wound, warn you of a coming storm, and bring a child from a flaming room. I can excel in danger, in a beauty parade, on a circus high wire, in a nursing home, on a lap. I am gifted. I can learn to win blue ribbons, be a best friend, and pose as hero before a camera. I can be the subject of a whole book, soften the spirit of a criminal, nurse a kitten, warm a climber on an ice ledge, run a sledge race and win. I am dog; I can feel pride and with you win a gold medal. Excellence will make for peace.

# Dear God,

*You have filled me with good things; you have made me gifted. Your own spirit is in me and I do in part what you do with power and glory. I can be to others what you are to me. Where there is danger I can save, where there is hunger I can feed, where there is a storm I can warn, where there is need I can be a hero. I have strength I have not tried and can teach what I have not yet learned. You have gifted me with passion I have not shown; filled me with music I have yet to sing and shown me excellence I have still to spend. Dear God, there are land mines I have yet to hunt, races yet to win and wounds to lick. You created all things excellent and there was peace in the garden. Your peace is hidden in all things.*

# Patient

**I am dog.** I will wait.

There is a time to run and time to lie down; there is a time to bark and a time to be still. Time can go fast or slow. Time can stretch long and stand still. Time can hurry. I keep time; everything around me keeps time. I cannot hurry sunrise; I cannot hurry rain; I cannot stop rain. When the rain stops I will run. I will wait for you to come home from work. I learn to know the length of a ride, a morning, a mealtime. I know the difference between three hours and a weekend. I prepare for when you leave; I know by how you talk to me, how you look at me, how you shut the door, drive away. I go to my water bowl; I know if you will be back soon or late. In this family everything has its time; I learn to keep my time. I am dog. Patience gives me peace. There are different kinds of time.

# Dear God,

*Sometimes I will not hurry. I will not run when I am already out of breath. I will not work when I am too exhausted. I will not lift what is too great a burden. I will go slowly. I will stop and rest. I may quit and surrender. I am not the timekeeper for all things, when to begin, when to finish. Peace requires patience. I am not in charge of time. There is a fullness of time I will learn to recognize the time we all keep. There is a right time for which I will wait. Patience will give me a new gait. Patience will help me see in all directions, feel feelings of others, know what to do next. Slow my feet and head and heart. Sometimes stop me to listen and look and hear what is right around me. Slow me down. Help me know what you have given that is in me. Walk me into peace.*

# Decide

**I am dog.** I will choose to do.

That is how it has always been; there is something I get to decide. When it comes to dog works I decide best. I am ready to be called into places where I can do the most good. Only I can hunt and rescue and dig and find with my ears and my good nose. This is how I am dog. I can quiet crying people, find the lost, guide the blind, save. Give me hard work to do and I will work. Send me into a disaster zone; I will decide where to run, when to sniff, where to stop, when to bark. There is work only dog does. I decide when the sun is high enough, when the day is dark enough. I tell you times of day, times of life. I decide when to run, when to hide, when to fight, when to growl, when to wean, when to romp, when to hunt, when to sleep. I decide from deep within where dog is dog. I watch the sun, the wind, the stars; I watch you. I will decide and you decide. I watch you watch me choose. There may be growling and then comes the peace. We choose together.

# Dear God,

*You have created me to choose. I can decide to do and not to do. I decide when to plant and when to reap, when to speak up and when to be still, when to shout and when to whisper, when to growl and when to sing. I know the disaster zones in the world, and will decide how I help and why I do not. I keep learning to say I will and I will not. There is a hurricane, I vote what to do. Death strikes, I vote; I experience sickness, divorce, loss, warfare, famine, flood and I decide; I vote. Miracles surround me, parables keep being told, and I decide if I will look to see them or listen to hear them. I vote. All those around me vote. I ask and see what they have voted, and the reason. May my growling prevent waging war. I will consider the meaning of all decisions for the sake of peace.*

# Honour

**I am dog.** I give honour.

I do not salute a flag. I salute you, your face, your voice, your presence, you. I will stand when you enter the room, greet you with dog protocol, and respect your every move. I will not act as though you are not present; I will give you worth for what you do that dog cannot do. You know a world I cannot feel and a world that is my mystery. You take me into your world as a best friend. I am dog; my world is a mystery. We see through the mystery and honour the maker of mystery. I honour you; you take me beyond yourself, beyond the mystery. I am dog; I bask in the mystery of being dog. You confound me with your being. I cannot salute you as you salute the flag. But I do respect, honour, and salute you for I am dog. I am loyal, respectful, graceful, tender, and great-hearted. I will rise when you enter the room, stay standing until you are seated. I will rise when you rise and face you. You are my flag.

# Dear God,

*I have learned to salute, pay tribute, revere and give honour. I know the sacred feeling in me when I stand for elders and for people famed. The gift of honour binds us. I feel the feeling of peace when I pay tribute to someone who does not expect honour or even being noticed. The nod of the head to a stranger on the high street, a slight wave of the hand noticing a passerby feels like a salute. I notice them with more than a glance and I feel the beginning of bonding with them. It is hard to think of them as enemy; the motion of the hand and nod of head is a sign of honour, respect, and relationship. I stand before another until I feel the honour. Every salutation is a sign of peace.*

# Cheer

**I am dog.** I can be a cheerleader.

If a howling breaks into the dark, I can keep it going. When it is too quiet I can start a solo in the dark. I can keep a Frisbee game running long after it's over. It is easy to turn a walk into a run, or a race. I can make you throw a stick once more when your arm is tired. I cheer you on with my heart and my tireless spirit. Throw a ball into the water, I will bring it to you and not quit. You know I will keep the game going one more time, and then one more. I cheer the tired, the sad, the weak and lonely. One move, one lick, one nuzzle, one more look and you are cheered. I am dog; I cheer you on and you are satisfied with laughter. We are at peace; we both won. Now we are quiet together. Put your hand on my head and we will both grow peace.

# Dear God,

*I did not know I could be a cheerleader, but I am.
I am learning to cheer for peace. More and more
I am out front, singing the songs, going through
the motions, saying the right words over and over,
shaping peace. People know that's what I do and who
I am. Some are shouting louder and louder with
me. Some sit silent. Some are on the other team with
the other opinion. My cheers are no angry words. I
do not embarrass the silent and offend the others.
My cheers seek truth, understanding, compassion,
prayer, reflection and petition. Peace does not come
by anger and rebuke and harassing. Peace comes by
uplifting the truth, the weak, the poor, and the tired.
I will not quit what will end in love. I cheer with
those who cheer me on. Peace is not grumpy. Keep us
cheerful when we cheer.*

# Hope

**I am dog.** I hope.

I hope for hours in silence, behind a shut door; on a doorstep I will wait, for you said you'd be back. I barked, begged; you promised. I can tell a promise that is being kept. My whole body feels when you are almost home, when you are almost awake, when we will soon take our walk. I am ready even before you say it is time. I bark when I hear the car in the driveway. I am in your way when you open the door. First you must notice me; then I will run ahead of you. If we will run or walk, I can tell. You do not ask me to follow twice; my hope prepares me to be alert, ready, half asleep, waiting, knowing for sure. You and I. You have kept your promise so I keep my hope. When you are ready, I am waiting at the door. I am dog. Hope is my bond. Your promise keeps hope from breaking. I am dog; I am ready to be with you. Who can ever separate us?

# Dear God,

*My peace is rooted in hope. Peace is an old story. I wait for goodwill, seek it and expect it. Nothing will separate me from the hope for peace. Nothing in heaven or earth will destroy my hope and expectation. Hope is your work among us, a force at work to bring beauty and balance and life to creation. Hope is not wishful thinking. Hope is built on old truth, old history, and the old word: Behold, everything is very good. Hope does not allow for the work of destruction and warfare and hunger and separation. Hope sees the oneness in creation, peace in nature, the singleness of heart, the unity of spirit, the family of all people. Bind us together with hope; link us in ways so we talk together, eat together, walk together, dream together, work together, live together. When we lose our way to peace, bring us back together through the law of hope.*

# Longing

**I am dog.** I long with all my heart.

I do not make valentines or send roses or write love letters. But you can see these in my eyes, in my

silence, in a bark whisper, a lick, a nuzzle, a loving whimper. My longing is like a love song. The sound is beyond me; it is not my own. I am silent so we both know, we both can tell, we are certain, there is no doubt. I long; only you can satisfy my wish. I am dog and my heart is insatiable. You know when to hold my face close, whisper, see in me. My heart is full. I give it to you the way dog gives. My valentine is bigger than my eyes show. See my face. You know longing; I am in your eyes. Nothing will erase my longing.

# Dear God,

*How my heart can long for peace. How my soul sometimes thirsts for a meadow with clear drinking water. There are in me songs of peace I have yet to sing. I know them by heart; I will sing them aloud. I will hear the hymns of peace around me and melodies beyond me. There are words and looks of peace near me on all sides. In the faces of needy and oppressed I see longing. I see the longing for rest, quiet, understanding, bread, good will, and peace. With psalmists and new singers I long; I want, and beg and wish. My heart is insatiable. Want has emptied me. Fill my longing heart with satisfaction. As you do this in me you do it to all your children. All want peace that comes when longing is stilled. We long; we wait and are fulfilled. We know the peaceful sound of your coming.*

# Marvel

**I am dog.** I marvel.

I can be amazed, dumbfounded, and caught flat-footed. There are times I stand staring, eyes blinking, disbelieving, stunned, flabbergasted, and marvelling. All you see is my silence; I am in a freeze like a mime. Still, like frozen. Slowly I move to show my hidden amazement and delight. I wag my tail, raise my ears, lift my head, and I touch you. One word can overwhelm me; I bark, once, barely. The marvel wakens in me: dancing, jumping, running in circles, frenzy. I marvel in silence; look, see the wonder in my eyes. I marvel in ecstasy. I like being overjoyed, amazed, and stunned to obedience. I am dog; there is much beyond me, outside me, within me that stirs marvel. I am not known to worship; not all is known of me. I am dog. I marvel and am fulfilled. My paw is touching you.

## Dear God,

*Help us stand together on tiptoe and marvel. Help nations see dreams for each other. Show leaders the glory in other lands. Blink our eyes with what each other does and thinks and imagines. Turn our wonder and amazement into worship, so all hearts come together in a single will for grace and peace. Draw us to what is far beyond and is deep inside so we are overwhelmed. Help us move beyond our selves. Show us resources inside ordinary places, in the poor, the hurt, so we build each other up as sisters and brothers. These are more precious than fine jewels. Today I will reach out to touch someone in thought or word to show wonder and thanks. We will be still that we may know you are one God and one peace.*

# Natural

**I am dog.** I am natural.

I have not learned pretence. What you see is what you get. If I lick your face to wake you, that is how I am. I will scratch myself before dinner guests and wag against their feet while they sit in sofas. If they let me I will sit near them on a pillow as I do when I am alone. If the door bell rings I may bark in the middle of sacred story. They may think I am at fault; the doorbell made me do it. It is who I am. I have been known to jump against people with suits and silk dresses. It is my friendly way. They look down at me, smile, say my name; I jump. I am dog; it is my natural way. Guests are welcome to this house. If they come again they will know me. We will learn to know each other. I am dog. I cannot do what they do. I am dog with all my heart. This is how I am made to be. I am created dog. Dog is my nature. I am here that we might have peace.

# Dear God,

*Your good news is my good news. Your gift of who I am is in me from the beginning. On every side are signs of who I am, who we are, who you are. I have memorized the story of who I am. I review the story of my nature. The garden of my beginning is a sacred place from my childhood. Often it was told to me. I see your peace in all that was to live around me. You made the garden and everything in it very good. The goodness and peace are hidden but not destroyed. Show me your peace in a wounded, warring world. Show our nations and neighbours how you have created us to befriend each other and all nature. Remove from me what distorts the goodness of others. Let not customs and perspectives of other people erase their worth and nearness to me. You know their hearts; you know them by name. You know who we are, how we are and why we are. Give us the peace that is shaped by our uniqueness, for we are many members and one body. Here I am Lord; you know me. It is so for us all.*

# Remember

**I am dog.** I remember.

    I still feel how you saved me from the cold, how you fed me when hungry, touched me when I returned, held me after being lost. I remember and you will save me again. You still want to call me, feed me, and welcome me with affection. I remember the rug I am allowed to lie on, a room that is not mine, an eating table I am not permitted to visit and my very own bowl. I remember rules; I remember affection. I remember when I was hurt and you asked me for pardon. I know what makes me cringe, when I am frightened, when I am neglected. I remember the seasons, the smell of autumn, the clap of thunder, and I know footsteps to the door by heart. I am dog; I remember what makes me be dog and be at peace.

# Dear God,

*You are a remembering God. You have built memory into creation. Seasons know when to come and go. Blossoms know when to bud and seed. You ask us to remember you and you will be there. This is how we stay near each other. In the clap of thunder, in the smell of springtime and a cry of a newborn we hear you at the door. In a sip of wine and breaking of a piece of bread we are at table with the universe and you are host. In a single thought loved ones in distant places, and gone ahead, are here. You have gifted us with the wonder of remembering. In the dark of night we remember in prayer those many who are foe and friend, those at war against our daughters and sons, and we remember them all in prayer. In remembering we find peace: the sick are near, we touch the weak, we forgive the enemy, and we dream with the old, we bless presidents and queens. Dear God, we are your remembering children.*

# Prevail

**I am dog.** I prevail.

I can hold out, out
beg, out smart and out last.
Surrender is not my strength.
I prevail with my eyes, my
bark, a whine, and presence.
It will stay and not move

until it is done. I will scratch a door to open until
I have won, and I will pay the consequence. I will run until I
am home. Though you tell me a hole is empty, I will dig until
I am convinced with my own eyes and nose. If I am to follow
a scent only you will stop me. I am insatiable. Deter me too
soon and I will return tomorrow, to insist, persevere, remind
you, persist. I am dog. I am made to seek, hunt, find and I
hold my head high like a winner. So I see you at the close of
good day: had a full day, feeling fine, got a lot done, good job,
finished the work. I am dog; count on me to prevail.

# Dear God,

*I will not give up. You are a persistent God. Your mercy prevails, your love wins, and your patience holds out, your peace will come. Your spirit is in me; I too pursue peace. Peace is a power, a strength, a determined heart, a work. Peace is not neutral, peace is not surrender; peace persists, prevails, wins. I will follow the path of peacemaking, for it will take me through valleys and shadows and desolation and battlefields and hospitals and bombings and death. Peace prevails to the very end. Peace is the blessing that sanctifies life and the last breath. Dear God, your peace is beyond understanding. Peace does not surrender or back off but enlists our minds and hearts to the end of time. Peace is the final word. Peace has the final say for peace is love.*

# Forgive

**I am dog.** I forgive.

A grudge will lead to isolation. Anger is my enemy; fear is a foe. I do not sleep well when we hurt. Forgiveness has the feel of stretching, a cool drink on a hot day, a warm blanket when chilled by rain, a safe pat after being chased by a predator. I cuddle without a word and come close with but a nod. Forgiveness gives me power, and I pass it around. My whole body shows forgiveness. It is no secret. Fear and anger hide; forgiveness is alive and is a force through my whole being. You will see me running with forgiveness from a distance. I have been waiting for the moment to bark and shake and paw when I am kindly. I know what you say and do to forgive. In a single moment I know: a touch, a morsel, a kiss, a sound, a whistle. Forgiveness is the highest rule.

# Dear God,

*I know your word: Thou shalt not hold a grudge.*
*Grudge is an enemy to peacemaking. Forgiveness is*
*stronger than fear and anger and grudge and harm.*
*Forgiveness breaks the strength of sin, the chain of*
*death and opens every kind of grave. Forgiveness*
*finishes a war, makes foe a friend and saves life. Dear*
*God, your forgiveness relaxes, is restful, quiets panic*
*and builds trust. My world needs your forgiveness,*
*and for us to forgive one another and ourselves. O*
*the power and the glory you have created in the act of*
*forgiveness. Forgiveness drew the prodigal back home.*
*Forgiveness is your master key to peace on earth.*

# Commitment

**I am dog.** I am committed to you.

I will keep my promise to you. I will do what we have agreed. If needed I will suffer for you, and be wounded in your stead. Do you know those many times when I would give you my life? If I hold back and do not guard you it is because the battle is too great for me. But in my heart I would defend you so that no harm overtakes you. My commitment is greater than my works. There is much I would do if I knew the way. I am dog and I commit the way dog commits. I keep my word; dog keeps a promise. Sometimes my great silence is my peace with you that is beyond my understanding. There is a tie that binds us which cannot be broken.

# Dear God,

*The cross is my sign of total commitment. There is a way that leads all the way. There is way for not backing off, not quitting in my heart. I will keep my promise as you have given yours to me. It is one promise and one commitment. I will do what we agree to do. If I am wounded in making peace I will go on. There is no battle too great for me. I will defend what is human and right and just with my whole heart. I do not yet know my limits; I do not know all there is to do. Tell me when I have finished. Show me some fruit of my works so I take heart and will not quit. If I am wounded make me well and send me on. The way of peace is a hard road. I will be your disciple.*

# Obey

**I am dog.** I obey.

Obedience is not a sign of weakness. I collaborate, cooperate. We agree with another. A joy builds in me when I obey. The obedience does not take advantage of me; it is a gift we have for each other. In a dog sledge race, I obey. There are rules I have learned by which we win. I cannot win without you or you without me. Obedience is our yoke. To live in a kennel with others I will obey. I am dog. We eat from the

same hand and are guided by the same yell. When learning to win a race I obey rules to qualify. I will hold the rules to the finishing line. To obey feels good and tastes good if it is a treat from your hand. Obedience knows a delight that is sweeter than sweets.

## Dear God,

*Teach me to obey. Kneel me at some rock and say in prayer "Your will be done." Give me a work in which I must obey to do the work well. Hold me close to you so our work can be done. Put me on my own while I am your apprentice. Jesus knew the steps of obedience. Teach your daughters and sons each step of the way, the craft of peacemaking, and the will to obey. Peace is not an easy work. Good will is crafted in all ways of life. We are in a race. We know the voice that cheers us along the run. Keep our eyes on the prize that is before us and is already in us.*

# Wander

**I am dog.** I wander.

I go off on my own and gather burrs in my fur. I do not notice soft mud rise above my feet; I only feel the cool pond, moist bog, the pleasure I have now discovered. This is my time to chase a butterfly and not be embarrassed that it escapes and laughs down at me. Wandering is fun as I pounce on a frog that happens in my way. This is not a hunt. I am dog meandering, on a stroll on a lazy summer day or in a windy wintertime. I am dog-catching snowflakes that bathe my eyes then disappear in the fall. I wander, noticing a family of birds and beasts here before me. I wander; I sniff and know their names. I romp through a maze of grouse and hare and mice and robins and ducks who have wandered here before me. The earth is a boundless garden of flowers and asphalt and steel and woods where I meander freely, and stray, and know my way home.

# Dear God,

*I stray and I know my way home. I have peace and then forsake peace. Sometimes I wander through a maze and am lost; there are times the maze leads me to hidden meadows and nooks and niches that become vistas. Tiny places where I find the still voice of God. Thank you for the gift of wandering and straying and returning. You made me free to come and go, to flee and come home barefoot and without your ring. I inherit a new ring. There are far off places I know by heart because you have set my heart loose and kept me in voice distance. All the earth is a wandering people, pilgrims on foot finding the path to the one place where all can be at the table eating one food and drinking one cup and passing the kiss of peace.*

# Watch over

**I am dog.** I guard.

I make safe. I will sleep with one eye to keep guard. I will hold my breath and count before deciding my attack. It is best not to engage in a battle I cannot win. I am dog and do not enjoy fleeing a foe in your presence. I too feel humiliation and do not like to be deceived. It is best to know one's own size and strength. Growling can be my best defence and ward off warfare. I have also found that wagging the tail and a soft greeting can calm the air. The enemy may only be a curious bystander, or a friend you know whom I have forgotten. I am dog and I watch you to see if you need guarding. If not, I will stay sleeping or I will follow you with your friend. Let me know you are safe and I will stay asleep.

# Dear God,

*You are with and in and among us. And you are over us. You are here and there and we know not quite where. Your rainbow is our constant sign of peace. All creatures, all creation, all people live under the one rainbow. You keep watch, you do not sleep, you protect. You are the one on high, the God on high over us. While you are in a manger of hay and a temple and two or three gathered, you are also over all. You are the blanket, the comforter, the cover in the cold, the dome of earth's cathedral and the seed before the oak. I too keep watch and shield and cover and protect and guard and keep. Night and day the world covers each other with intercession and kindness. Peace is a shield, a quilt, and the work of guardian angels. Dear God, your own Holy Spirit is the great comforter from on high. Earth is filled with a spirit of peace.*

# Lead

**I am dog.** I go ahead; I lead the way.

I am often a forerunner; I plot, plan, and probe in my way. It is not a straight line for I know side roads and byways. I know the high road and the low road. I am dog and can run both roads at once. I know the slow ways that dawdle and we stand still. I know the fast slopes and fence lines and we chase. I lead with all my senses; as birds migrate the sky I span the landscape. I will lead the blind so they see; I am a quiet guide who keeps you safe in a maze and you go as on your own. I am dog; I go ahead as a messenger, barking glad tidings that we are back home. They will know you are near for I have run to tell them.

# Dear God,

*We all have forerunners, those who lead the way. There are the saints and martyrs who probed and loved and lived and died before us. They still lead us. They know a high road we have yet to travel. They rest in peace and their peace is still at work. We too lead. That same peace is our peace for there is one peace, your peace. We all run the race with a candle given us long ago, lighted at baptism. Make me a gentle guide who leads and does not chase, who goes ahead to show peace. I will skip while I run. Dear God, I will lead from within, alongside as walking, ahead as a light upon the path, running as a herald. Peace is not just the end of the way; the journey is the peacemaking.*

# Laugh

**I am dog.** I laugh.

I can tell when something's a joke; I am dog; look close, I have a sense of humour. I like things that don't seem to fit. If you eat from my bowl, see me notice. Curl up on my rug and I jump all around the room. Imitate my walk and I can go into ecstasy. Ride me on the handlebars of the bike and I hold my breath from laughter. I am dog. Pretend to bark and talk my language, and I tremble and wag with joy at your accent. You say one thing and I hear another; if you only knew what I am hearing you say. Our worlds overlap with the mystery of enjoyment. You go into detail with words and signs; I laugh. Your antics to me are full of oxymorons. You do not always know why or when I laugh. Listen, look and notice how much fun I think you are. You are my comedian in residence. My body is filled with joy.

# Dear God,

*Why am I so often laughing? Why do I have this sense of humour? What is your greatest joke? What is it that makes people smile the most? Is it the face of a camel or the feet of a kangaroo? Or is the joke your grace? Is love and grace and peace the big joke, the big surprise, the most joyful idea on earth? Your peace that passes all understanding makes the world smile and laugh and sing and praise. Peace is the great puzzle you have given your children. Peace is the riddle we are here to solve. Dear God, you are theologian, gardener, judge, and singer. You are the comedian of the world. Sometimes we catch on, sometimes not, often later. Then we laugh. What does not fit becomes your rule. Sinners are saved; this calls for laughter. Grace is your great sense of humour. Peace is your big puzzle.*

# Heal

**I am dog.** I heal.

I know when a wound needs a lick, when a tear needs a snuggle, and when to come close to you. I know what is too close and too soon. I am dog and will wait outside your door if you are isolated. You know I am there. When you want good news I am your good news. When you want thumbs up I look you in the face and declare you well. I do not see you as sick; I see you as getting well. I bring a rag or chewed bone to test your spirit. I am ready to play; you are not and I will wait. I am dog and remind you of good times and how we made it before. I cannot reach the medicine chest, but I bring you what the chemist cannot bottle. I am dog, more than a prescription drug. National Health cannot afford me and I come free to you. One whistle, one look and I am at your side. Touch me, hold me and be well.

# Dear God,

*I too make people well. I tend plants and feed birds. I visit sick, bring flowers you grow, tell them good news, and bring our one hope. We praise your doctors and thank your nurses. We learn the names of those who draw our blood and marvel how they read the meanings of signs inside us which eye cannot see. In surgery people from all lands in garments of blue and white surround us and serve to heal us. Though our lands are at war all healers together are your angels. There is no enemy in the room of healing. I am alone, a friend calls. I am depressed, someone comes to talk. I am sick; a prayer chain is at work. I believe, you make me well. Dear God, the whole earth is of one mind; we all want to be well. Peace is also being well.*

# Judge

**I am dog.** I can judge.

I can vote on how it is with you, your mood, and your spirit. Your tone of voice can slow me.

I take one more look at how it is with you. I weigh. I am dog and I balance both ends. I see left and I look right and know the middle, the centre. I am dog and you will not be confused or tricked. I can learn tricks but will not be tricked. You are innocent until guilty a few times. I can hold you on probation and make you accountable. Stay near me and grow honest. Walk with me and I will hear you; run with me and I will set you free. I am dog; I will be your advocate. Only ask. Peace requires a verdict.

## Dear God,

*I vote. In my crib I voted. In my mother I did vote.
I am made to keep going, to move on; there is a goal.
I am on a journey and will not be tricked. I cannot
travel this road without wisdom and judgment.
Every turn and day I decide, vote, judge. I weigh
which way to turn, which words to say, which cause
to condemn, which work to support. I will make
judgments with my spirit, with word and tone of my
voice, with simple deeds. I will be held accountable;
my heart will be a jury. I will listen, love, care,
understand. You are my rock, my fortress, my Yes and
Amen. I will be the same. You will give me words to
speak. Run with me and I will hear you, walk with
me and we will talk, stay with me and I will break
your bread. When I vote, we vote. Peace demands
judgment.*

# Follow

**I am dog.** I can follow.

I can tag along and loiter while you will lead the way. You can be in charge. I will dawdle, linger, investigate, sniff my way, zigzagging. I will hear you whistle, calling me on, waiting, wishing me to follow. You lead and I will follow. I am not afraid to be far behind; you will not leave me. You know I will follow, eventually, because when you are leading then I am not. I know the feeling of following. The safe feeling of not knowing where I am going and you know. You will not forsake me. I fall far behind; you call, I hear you but you do not see me. I am not ready to hurry; you come back to find me, call me, coax me, and lure me on. I follow the way I follow. On a leash I am close behind you, at your side, or just ahead. On my own I follow, for you will lead. When I do not know the way you know the way. I am dog. I follow for I trust. We arrive together.

# Dear God,

*I too tag along, sometimes dawdle, and linger but I will follow. You will not leave my sight. I will learn to follow on a way I do not yet know. There is a tomorrow I cannot see and a bend in the road I cannot know. The road may be severe. I will chart my journey; I will remember landmarks, mark milestones, record holy days. The way is well marked. Multitudes have travelled this road before me. Their footprints are fresh, benchmarks are set to song, old pilgrims keep stories alive, children still dance and shout hosanna. Dear God, I will follow. I will stay close. My mind is a disciple's mind; I will keep my thoughts on you. You do not let me out of your sight. I do not know the way; you are the way. My feet are dressed in peace.*

# Celebrate

**I am dog.** I celebrate.

I can move every part of my body at once in a dance. I can make a little go a long way. Give me a crumb or a sip and I can make it a party. It will look as though we have had a banquet together. One pat and I will thank you forever. One word of kindness and I will go an extra mile. A little is enough to keep me going. Throw a stick and I will run in cold or heat and bring it to your feet. If I tire it is still party time. I can go beyond my old limits if we are smiling. Laugh and I will do an encore. Give me a treat and I will do two encores. Hug me and I will not count the encores. I was born of a family tree that finds pleasure, and in a family where we romped and tumbled the first day. We did not wait to be invited to go to some playground. Our mother was our playground. I am dog. Celebrating is an instinct. You are my peace candle.

# Dear God,

*You created celebration. You began the work with a great light. We still light candles. We light them for birthday, birth, death, wedding, and the wake. Candlelight is the promise of your nearness and presence. Candlelight is the signal for a song and sacrament. One balloon and children begin the dance. We are marked to celebrate. Celebrating is a gift of the Spirit. All generations have sung their psalms and flown their homemade kites. Gloria in Excelsis is the song of children learning to read, of mothers musing, choirs rehearsing, lovers dreaming, babies nursing, angels singing, and people dying. Dear God, in a piece of bread shared you have hidden glory, in a seed buried you have hidden a garden, in an acorn fallen you have hidden a forest; in Jesus you have hidden yourself. So be in me that I may be at peace in the world.*